Hardwired
and
Ready to Go

Miracles, Faith, and a
Glimpse of the Afterlife

Hardwired and Ready to Go

By Dave Seidel

Copyright © 2024 Dave Seidel

All rights reserved. No part of this book may be reproduced or transmitted in any form or by any means, electronic or mechanical, including photocopying, recording or by any information storage and retrieval system, without written permission from the author, except for the inclusion of brief quotations in a review.

First Edition 2024

ISBN 13: 978-1-952685-94-1

Edited by Reprospace, LLC
Cover Design by Reprospace, LLC

This is a work of fiction. Names, characters, places, and incidents either are the product of the author's imagination or are used fictitiously. Any resemblance to actual persons, living or dead, events, or locales is entirely coincidental.

Kitsap Publishing
Poulsbo, WA • USA

This book is dedicated to my longsuffering wife, Janice Elaine Seidel who with God's grace, has survived a brain tumor for 27 years and is still going strong.

And also to my oldest grandchild, Rachel Mae Seidel, who challenged me to write my "grandpa stories" and then recorded my first outline for the book while I was recovering from triple bypass surgery.

Acknowledgement

Special thanks to Larry D. Peabody who arranged a meeting so I could record my special vision and then later edited my manuscript and expressed wonderful encouragement.

David D. Seidel

Foreword

by the Publisher

When I first encountered David Seidel's story, I was struck by its honesty, depth, and the way it resonates with anyone who has ever faced life's hardships head-on. *HARDWIRED and Ready to Go* isn't just a series of events; it's a journey through moments of profound faith, resilience, and the unwavering belief that we are connected to a greater purpose.

David's experiences are both humbling and inspiring. He's walked paths that many would find daunting, and he's done so with a quiet strength that can only come from true faith. His story speaks to those who, at times, may feel overwhelmed or alone, offering comfort in the reminder that, even in our darkest moments, there's a light at the end of the tunnel guiding us forward.

What I find most powerful about this book is its warmth and accessibility. David's words have a way of reaching out, inviting us to see ourselves in his journey and to reflect on our own sources of strength and meaning. His story isn't about having all the answers but about the courage to keep searching, to keep believing, and to trust in the connections that lift us up.

As you read, I hope you find the same sense of hope and encouragement that I did. David's story reminds us all that faith, love, and resilience can carry us through life's most difficult challenges, and that we are never truly alone.

Ingemar Anderson—Kitsap Publishing, Poulsbo, WA

Table of Contents

Foreword
Preface
I. Early Insecurities — 1
II. Finding God's Direction for My Life — 5
III. More Direction Just Before College — 10
IV. College, Marriage, and Seminary — 17
V. Back to the Pacific Northwest — 24
VI. Helping in a Rural Church — 27
VII. Chris Has a Stroke — 30
VIII. Mount St. Helens — 33
IX. Shane Breaks a Wrist — 37
X. Cars for Missionaries Project — 39
XI. Heather's Miraculous Recovery From SCAD — 43
XII. Jan's Twenty-seven Year Ordeal — 46
XIII. The Surgeries — 50
XIV. Jan's Seizure and Broken Clavicle — 52
XV. Goodbye Equinox and Hello Prius — 56
XVI. Proton Therapy for Jan and Dave's Need for Surgery — 59
XVII. Dave's "Tunnel Vision" — 65
XVIII. Love Sent Me Back — 71
XIX. Going Home — 73
XX. The Zoom Meeting Grace Adult Class — 75
XXI. The Sketch and Painting — 78
XXII. Aftermath — 79
XXIII. Conclusion — 81
Seven Take Aways — 84
Works Cited — 85

Preface

Connectivity is a big deal these days. It has become rather routine for us to keep our cell phones plugged in and powered up. A day hardly passes that we do not power up to energize something from phones to our vehicles, computers, and electronic games. One of the greatest challenges facing modern technologists is the development of more powerful batteries, because no one wants to run out of power. I suppose it should not come as a surprise that finite beings wrestle with finding an infinite power source.

My youngest grandson, Maverick, was sitting in my living room, about to plug in his game machine. He looked up and said, "Papa, do you know where the best place to play my game machine is?" Now, I had to qualify his inquiry. "Do you mean the quietest or the place your machine works best? "He simply replied, "Where I get the most power." My interest was piqued and I told him, "Yes, I would like to know." He continued, "Well, it is right on the other side of the house."

Now I had a hunch it was in my office, because that is where the modem sits and feeds the Wi-Fi to the rest of the house. Maverick had discovered where his power source, the power to run his game machine best, came from, and he was not shy about powering it up as long and as often as his parents would allow. The modem has to be plugged in but ultimately the receptacle in the wall is "hardwired" to the house's main power supply.

What about our spiritual life, though? Isn't it just, or even more important, to make sure we keep hardwired into the one power supply that is constantly available to meet our every need? Now you may ask, just what does being "hardwired" entail? The preposition "into" gives away part of the answer. We use "into" to say that someone is interested in or involved with something. Being hardwired speaks of permanency and therefore demands a commitment and in this case a spiritual one. "Into" also suggests a change or transformation. As you read through the transformative experiences I have had and my family, keep an open mind to how you too can make sure you are hardwired into the life Jesus would have you live. If a ten-year-old, like Maverick, could identify his power supply and know how to power up, maybe we too can identify our spiritual power source and keep wired into Jesus.

I am writing to share with you how Jesus Christ has met, not only my needs but those of my family at critical times throughout our lives--and sometimes quite miraculously. Staying hardwired into a relationship with Jesus is not just important but critical if we are to realize our full spiritual development that God has planned for us.

The whole idea of relating this to you came to me while my granddaughter, Rachel Mae Seidel, was caring for me during my recovery from triple by-pass heart surgery. A few years earlier, she had given me a book of 1001 New York Times crossword puzzles by Will Shortz, because she knew puzzles were "my thing." After a dozen puzzles or so, I began to tell her some "Grandpa stories" and she said, "Papa you should write these down." I agreed, "Okay, but first we need a rough outline." She was kind enough to take down my rough outline for this book. At first, I thought, "How can I do this? Her writing is extremely small!" But after finding my magnifying glass, the outline was a great aid to me later. Now I can relate, in detail, the events that have caused me to feel hardwired into Jesus over the years but especially the last nine months. I will relate more about my recovery from heart surgery and "tunnel vision" experience.

PART ONE

I.

Early Insecurities

Growing up in the heart of the Inland Empire in Spokane, Washington, my childhood was a typical one. My parents sent my older brother and sister and myself to the neighborhood Sunday school and church but did not attend themselves. Sometime during elementary school, we stopped attending the local church. For some reason, I always felt guilty passing the church to play ball at the nearby playground. This guilt was heightened when I was bouncing a basketball on Sunday mornings and had to pass the place. The elementary school did release students who wished to attend a kid's Bible club at the church. While in that club, I was asked if I had a Bible at home and when I said no, they gave me one. It was very old and tattered so we made a book cover for it out of aluminum foil.

My Mother spoiled me, the youngest of her five. My Father was a hard-working, blue-collar plumber. He frequently called me any one of a variety of curse words, and by the time I started school, I was fortunate to discover I had a real name. Often, when my dad was drinking, you could find me playing sports at the local school yard. A good deal of the time, I felt insecure, and was not sure of my future.

My father's teaching was simple: decide what you believe in and then stick to it. This was before he came to belief in Christ shortly before he died. I remember him watching the preacher and evangelist, Oral Roberts, and saying, "There is something about him placing his hand on their foreheads and they are healed." It was by watching Billy Graham on a telecast that he made the decision to trust Jesus as his savior. I learned from my mother that he had attended church as a child but because he had not attended all year he was not rewarded with an orange and decided to never go back. It is too bad it took 60 years to get his spiritual life figured out. He became a Christian in the spring before he passed from Lou Gehrig's disease a year after he retired.

My Mother received much of her home remedy medical training from her Mother, my Granny. Her family had come from Missouri by way of the Ozarks in Tennessee where cod-liver oil and mustard plasters cure all types of ailments. Once when I was about ten my tonsils had become infected and my mother called my Granny to get some advice. The conversation went like this: Mother: "What shall I do? D.D.'s (my childhood nickname) tonsils are swelling and I am afraid he might choke to death and the drugstores are all closed." Granny: "Does Fred have any whiskey around?" Now this was a little like asking Popeye if he had any spare spinach. Mother: "Well, he just might." Granny: "Give him a tablespoon of that." I remember my mother coming at me with that tablespoon full of vile looking liquid. "What is that stuff?" I stammered. "Never mind just open up and swallow this," she demanded. I closed my eyes and gulped it down. Then I did not breathe for three minutes. "What—What was that stuff?" I stammered after catching more breath. She smiled and said, "Just medicine." By morning my tonsils were down and so I recovered. I thought at the time my mother had scared my tonsils into recovering. Since then, I learned the medicinal value of 90-proof Irish whiskey.

All three of my uncles served in the military during WWII. They also all had heart problems. Two lived in Clarkston, Washington, not far from my grandmother. They both were treated with little pink pills and lots of bed rest at the Veterans hospital in Spokane. Open-heart surgery had not yet been perfected in 1959 but I am sure they could have benefited by it. They both passed away that fall and winter and I vividly remember the twenty-one gun salutes and folding of the flags at the cemetery. This instilled a sense of permanency in my ten-year-old mind that did not help my insecurities. But later, would definitely play a part in my decision to follow Jesus Christ.

When I was in fifth grade a classmate who sat next to me was abducted and murdered, which added to my insecurity. It was not until a little over sixty years later that the case was solved and finally closed. Everyone that lived in Spokane from March 1959 and on was aware of this famous case. One Friday, we were playing baseball in front of the elementary school when someone on a bike shouted to us, "The Boy Scouts are gathering to look for Candy." Now there was only one Candy I knew of and she sat next to me that day in school. Rushing in the door at home, I immediately relayed the news to my mother, "All of Pack One is gathering to hunt for Candy. This is a big deal." She tried to console me and said, "Kids go missing all the time and then they turn up later. Do not worry one little bit. She will turn up." Her face, though, betrayed the words she was saying. As the weeks mounted, with no real leads, parents began to lock their doors and follow the story as it failed to unfold. Some hunters discovered her body after a few months. Then, with no new developments, the case was all but forgotten. It was only because of the breakthroughs in DNA forensics that the case was solved 62 years later.

My very first day in Junior High school my insecurities were further heightened. Some bully shoved my head in a locker and held it closed as long as he could. When I was finally able to stand up, I challenged him to meet me after school. Little did I know he was more than just some bully. He was the Northwest Golden Gloves boxing champ for his weight class. His father was a fight promoter and he had already had four ring fights and won all by knockouts. Word of the incident spread fast and suddenly I had no friends. After school I laid low on the sidelines at an upper-class football game. My opponent failed to show but he sent one of his stoolies by. He grabbed me by the collar and said, "Don't mess with Kelly." After my friends learned I was still living they did again associate with me, but not right away. It was only a few years ago I learned he had been held back in elementary school and was two years older than me. My misaligned thoughts of vengeance turned to forgiveness just realizing he had his own demons to overcome. Although Kelly was in my homeroom in High School things were never quite right between us. I learned in college that he had been killed in Vietnam while out on patrol. I hope he had an opportunity to get right with the Lord. They say there are no atheists in fox holes.

On through Junior High School trouble seemed to be my middle name. It was a strange time when teenage boys would craft wooden hack boards in woodshop class and give them to teachers to apply to the bottoms of the "naughtiest" of students. I think I had the school record -- twelve hacks in two years. Looking back, I was probably acting out because of my insecurities at home. Why this led me to throw a student in the shower with his clothes on I cannot really say. My punishment was a hack from the PE teacher. His board was the end of an oar handle with a ping pong paddle mounted to it. So, after a shower I received my hack in the nude from coach C. The paddle also had holes drilled through it. The effect was to leave welts on your rear end. One story that circulated claimed that a teacher in the Midwest missed and struck a student in the back paralyzing him. Although many states abolished this practice, as late as 2024, corporal punishment is legal in 17 states and practiced in 14 of them. Washington State banned corporal punishment in 1994.

The players on the school basketball team each recruited players for intermural teams and then a tournament took place. There were the lions, bears, tigers, and a few other animal named teams. My team was made up of the more ruffians of the school: Larry, Chuck, Pete, Richard, even Kelly and we were the scorpions. We tended to foul out a lot but did place third in the tournament.

School officials made me bathroom monitor during lunch periods. They apparently thought that they could use my observation skills to their advantage. Nearly every day I observed one boy would verbally insult another whose name was Chin. One day Chin, having been backed up against the wall, had heard enough and he suddenly grabbed the bigger boy and bounced his head off the large round wash basin. It was obvious from his stance that he was a student of martial arts and a very good one. "I am very sorry, very sorry, but I could not take another word," he stammered. I was not sure which one was in more shock. So, with blood running down the bigger boy's face, I grabbed a cold paper towel and he slapped it on and we all migrated down to the office.

About this time, my sister had started attending a Christian church with a neighboring family. It was not long until I was asked to ride along. The very first time I returned to Sunday

School my teacher asked if I would like to stay after class and I jumped at the chance to ask a few questions. He presented the gospel in a way I could understand and led me in a prayer in which I confessed my sins and asked Jesus to come into my life. Although he was fresh out of Canadian Bible College and not yet a pastor at the time, I will forever be indebted to Pastor Gene. Immediately I felt a huge weight was lifted off me. It was the difference between night and day. I no longer wondered if God really cared about me and I felt accepted and kind of like I was part of something much bigger than just myself. Soon I came to see how I now had a heavenly Father who would never let me down and I could count on him for direction in life's difficult circumstances. Not only did this young future pastor take me to a father and son dinner but other men in the church began to mentor me.

The verses we were sent home with, and asked to memorize, from the neighborhood church years earlier, began to make more sense to me now: John 3:16 and I John 1:9. "If we confess our sins, he is faithful and just and will forgive us our sins and purify us from all unrighteousness" (NIV). My favorite was Revelation 3:20. "Behold I stand at the door and knock. If any man hears my voice and opens the door, I will come in and sup with him and he with me" (KJV). My door was now wide open and I just needed a little direction to know how my life should unfold. My aluminum-foil covered bible was replaced by a Zondervan Chain of Reference Bible my older sister, Margie, bought for me and served me well through college and seminary.

II.
Finding God's Direction for My Life

My Junior year in High School my life took a serious turn. In the spring, in eastern Washington, many farmers gas their fields to kill ground squirrels and any ground dwelling menaces that might later jamb up their cultivating equipment. My friend, Ed, and I used this to approach a farmer from our church to allow us some hunting fun. Armed with a couple 22 rifles and a few boxes of ammunition we headed to Deer Park, a little north of Spokane, and received some last-minute instructions from the farmer. These instructions and directions culminated with him saying, "Don't shoot my cows in the next field over." We loaded the guns at the fence line and found a few cans to take a few target practice shots and then began walking the fields.

After nearly a full day of roaming the fields and nearby woods, we were both tired and had only managed to knock off a few ground squirrels, but we did avoid the cows roaming the woods. We decided to head home. Ed was older than I was by three or four years and much more experienced with weapons having just come from a tour of duty in the army. When we reached the fence line, we both unloaded our guns and headed for Ed's car. It was dusty and he had his rifle in one hand and his dusty shoes in the other.

As soon as I climbed in the front seat of his car, I heard a shot from the other side of the car. "Ed must have seen a last-minute ground squirrel," I thought to myself. Then I heard a sound that will forever be in my mind. I dashed around the car and found Ed spinning on the ground and then suddenly stop. I put my hand under him. The warm blood on my hand told me the bullet had gone clean through him. Later, I would learn that while placing the rifle behind the front seats, and having the other hand occupied with his shoes, he had attempted to flick the safety with his toe and came down on the trigger. The bullet he left in the rifle's chamber had ripped through his body from one side and out his opposite back shoulder. So much for trying to practice safety.

The farmer had heard the shot, saw what was happening, and quickly went in action. He yelled at his wife to call the Deer Park hospital emergency and tell them we were coming in with a gunshot victim. We piled Ed in the back of the farmers VW bug and headed to the hospital. It seemed like we would never get there and Ed was breathing fast but clearly unconscious. In between my mental prayers I explained to the farmer what I believed had happened. They were waiting for us at the emergency door and quickly rushed him in. After a short-time a hospital staffer said that since the bullet went through his body, where critical organs were located, it was highly likely he would not survive the operation he would need. Ed needed a major miracle if he were to live. They were rushing blood from Spokane for the operation. I was so scared, and I am still not sure just how I made it home.

After I explained to my parents what had happened, I washed my bloody hand and tried to eat while anxiously listening for the phone to ring. Never in my young life did I pray harder.

By this time the news of the accident had spread to Garland Avenue Church and a special prayer meeting was called for Ed's recovery. Finally, after a few hours, the phone rang and Ed's father explained how the bullet had bounced off his stomach, collapsed one lung and just missed his heart. Then it exited his back shoulder. The surgeon told Ed's father this was the only path, on this trajectory, the bullet could take without hitting his heart or other organs. If Ed survived the night he would be out of the woods and might recover completely.

Suddenly, I realized how tired I was and almost forgot to hang up the phone. My mother seemed even more relieved than I as she told me to go up to bed. Soon she followed and shoved my bible under my pillow. I was too tired to read, but I remember praying that if God would heal my friend, I would do anything He wanted me to do. Later, I learned I did not need to try to bargain with God but I could make my request known to Him and He would always be listening.

The next morning my brother, Bill, retrieved from Ed's car his 22 I had borrowed. Bill was eight years my senior, and had previously assured my mother that I was pretty level headed, and the accident was surely not my fault. Ed did recover and in three weeks was up and around. I asked him what it felt like to be shot. He said it was like someone poked a hot coat-hanger through him. Just a couple months later, Ed had colitis and required another operation. Recovering in the convalescent home, I visited him on my way home from school. He got down to 88 pounds and again the church prayer team and I prayed for God to heal him. This group of prayer warriors would wear out the floor when they got down, literally, to praying. Then a most unusual thing happened.

No, a bolt of lightning did not hit Ed and heal him. A man named Dutch, who weighed nearly 300 pounds in the bed next to him, suddenly died. Ed became determined not to let this happen to him. He began drinking malts and putting on weight. He was released to go home after he was feeling better and had gained some weight. I lost contact with Ed, but learned he had studied medicine at the University of Oregon and had become an inhalation therapist. He could strap on a special belt to protect his colectomy bag so he and his son could do club boxing.

III.
More Direction Just Before College

This whole experience caused me to change my direction from heading off to Officer Candidate School in the Coast Guard to Bible College and seminary. God was directing my path and within a year an even more personal experience would challenge my commitment to follow him.

My youth advisor and future brother-in-law had attended Simpson Bible College in San Francisco and his input was a big factor in my choosing to apply there. I was accepted my Senior year but had no job, not much experience, or much money. I did have something even better than these. Lots of people were praying for me. A head hunter for a personnel company attended my church and helped me find my first job after I graduated from high school. It was at a combination gas station and fuel oil company. Since it was way across town, I would need to take three buses to get there. Now my father had already signed up to take my older sister to her job at the downtown library and pick her up. So, with this experience freshly in mind, he decided to buy my first car, a 1952 Plymouth sedan for forty dollars. Little did I know it would nearly take my life.

To say I was hard on this car was an understatement. Frequently my date would have to help me push it just to get it started. Thank heavens it was not an automatic and could be started in compression. Late one night, and only a couple weeks from needing to leave for school, I lost the muffler on the 52. I guess I thought that it was a little loud but I would fix it later. One morning, it was cold and I rolled all the windows up. Besides, it was loud. Within 30 minutes of getting to work I began to get very dizzy and suddenly half my body froze up and I cried out, "Lord help me", collapsed and went unconscious. When I woke up, I tried to get up but two people were holding me down. They were ambulance attendants who loaded me up and rushed me to St. Lukes hospital near my home.

The hospital ran some heavy-duty tests to rule out major problems: electroencephalograph; spinal tap; various x-rays; and dexterity tests (watch my finger stuff). They concluded I seemed alright but later may want to have an angiogram to rule out a brain tumor. I forgot to tell them about my missing muffler and don' t recall them taking my blood to test for that. My mother and I committed this to the Lord, thinking it must have been the carbon monoxide. My parents and I left for Bible College in San Francisco the next Friday. We both felt peace about this decision and it never bothered me again. I felt I had an invisible power supply for strength that was just beyond me.

Just so my three kids and their ten kids and anyone interested want to know what happened to my 52 Plymouth split window, here is what happened. After my parents drove me to college in San Francisco, my dad came home and sold the car to some kids from WSU for 65 dollars. This amazed me at the time because I had struck another car and completely bomb canned the pea green Plymouth to royal blue with about twelve cans of spray paint. My friend Ed came by the next morning and laughed his head off. The third member (rear differential) had to be replaced with my brawn and my dad's guidance. I never told him I had popped the clutch and it was entirely my fault I ruined the rear end.

In 1966 it was getting a little difficult to find a rearend for a 52 Plymouth, but I was able to locate one. Ed and I headed out to the wrecking yard and paid twenty-five dollars for one. While we were there Ed spotted his old 57 Ford that he had wrecked on Deadman's curve out on North Wall Street a few years before. We took a few minutes to look inside and Ed retrieved a few school pins from the sun visors and I got his old seat covers that now matched my freshly sprayed Plymouth.

Just after this, on an early summer fishing trip, another friend and I decided to find the perfect spot and followed a little creek up a mountain not far from Mount Spokane. As we approached the top of the mountain, suddenly it just ended. It ended so fast that I did not see a big rock sticking up in the middle of the road and we ran onto it and the fan put a hole in the radiator. We found a bucket in the trunk and were able to keep filling the radiator as we drove down. We would stop and refill the radiator every half mile or so. We were traveling too fast and began to brodie around the gravel curves. I turned once to the wrong side and we flew off the road into a ditch. I tried to get back on the road but got stuck coming up. We had passed a ranger about a mile back and were sure he was going to come after us so we cooked up a good plan. We would shovel out behind the rear tire and say the road had caved in. After about half an hour we realized the ranger was not coming. It was clear we had literally reached the end of the road but it was not clear what we should now do.

My friend, Larry, had a great idea. He remembered a farm we had passed on the way in. He would hike ahead and see if someone could help us. Meanwhile I filled the radiator again and waited and prayed. It was not long and I saw Larry return with a farmer riding a big tractor. We pulled the car back on the road, thanked the farmer and even repaired the road. Well, sort of. Then we were off again on the way home.

Soon we realized the back tire had gone flat. We were sure it must be a manufacturing defect. We began to change the tire and remembered we had already used the spare tire. We would have to travel to the next station to have it repaired traveling on the flat. Now we had turned onto the paved main highway. When we finally reached a service station a worker there asked, "how far have you come on that flat?" Now there was nothing left of the tire but a few strands of casing. "About twenty miles," we sheepishly replied.

So, we had the first spare repaired and mounted on the car and headed off again. Soon we heard a slight knocking from the engine and then it quit. We had forgotten about the hole in the radiator. Without enough water, the engine had over heated and froze up. We were on a paved road, in the middle of nowhere, wondering if this was the end of the road for our little fishing adventure. We flagged down a flatbed truck and the driver gave us a lift back to Spokane.

Now I was fortunate to have a friend named Ray who had just returned from the Navy. He agreed to help me get the 52 back to Spokane. We were able to borrow a 42 Ford flatbed truck from my filling station job because we were, after all, only a few miles out of town. It was about 30 miles back to the car. Ray drove the truck and we placed a tire between the vehicles on a large tow rope. The truck had no lights so we had to be careful and quick. We did make it back and turned in the truck just before the station closed. They wondered if we were ever coming back.

Dad, being the good old school plumber he was, used his lead pot to fill the hole and with a good deal of radiator Stop Leak it did not leak a drop. So, all in all, yes, my dad had negotiated an amazing deal when he sold it to some students from WSU for sixty-five dollars.

Through all of this, God was preparing me for some kind of ministry and I wanted to remain as open as possible. My youth advisor, Ken Cole Sr., had told me once that although you go to Bible College and perhaps on to a seminary, "If you are too heavenly minded you may become no earthly good." I filed this information away, along with how to place a side body block on your basketball opponent. Anyone who knew Ken knows what I am talking about. For someone who once tried to guard Elgin Baylor at Seattle University, it seemed, at times, like Ken was running in football shoes in the gym. Ken had a terrific sense of humor. Once he was driving me home from a youth meeting and when we came to the turn onto West Boone from Ash Street, he let the wheel slide between his fingers and said, "Dave, I don't know if I can make it." I was scared out of my wits and quite white knuckled. Of course, we made the turn and I learned Ken had a more than robust sense of humor.

My father-in-law, Lewis Cole, was one of my biggest mentors. He once gave me three important elements to discovering God's will for one's life: (1) By reading the Bible and praying and asking God to take full control; (2) You will often have an inner desire to accomplish something and peace about doing it; And (3) scripture will often confirm your decision to proceed in a certain way. It is amazing how many times these three elements lined up for me and then circumstances occurred that took me in a certain direction. Now this was advice that I could really value and apply. His son's advice about side-body blocks--well, not so much.

IV.

College, Marriage, and Seminary

As my grades the first few years in college reflected, I spent more time in the gym and on the basketball court than on studies. I barely knew where the school library was until the second semester of my freshman year. On a basketball tour up to the Portland Oregon area, the team was staying at our denominations camp in Canby near Portland. The team was divided up playing football on a field with an old softball diamond. We had been traveling all morning and it was good to be out exercising a little. I had just caught a pass and decided to jump over the few boards left of the softball backstop. What I did not see was the fine netting that had been stretched between the taller boards. The netting caught my face and my feet went straight forward. I came down on the lower boards with my neck and I thought I had broken it. My face and nose were chewed up as well. I laid down in one of the cabins and after aspirin and a nap felt much better. The whole team and business manager were praying for me and I think it really was the difference because I was able to play ball the next day. We ended up splitting the games on tour and went back to school to heal up.

Now it usually takes something intense to end a college tradition. Late one night I had just finished walking Jan back to her dorm when I noticed strange movements behind trees and bushes. I took off running and soon ten or twelve guys were right behind me. I thought maybe I could make it down a hill and to my car beside the school. Just then someone stepped out behind a tree and I went head over heels. Soon I was at the bottom of a dog-pile.

The custom was to catch the guys getting engaged take them down to the gym, strip them down and smear them with peanut butter. Each year the initiation evolved a little and more creative elements were employed. One young engaged guy received a heart and arrow shape with indelible ink on his buttocks. I was the first of the season and because I had been quick to help as an underclassman, they figured I would help get the rest. At one point I broke free and almost escaped into one participant's Ford Falcon Ranchero but missed a door lock on one side and got pulled out again. I was taken about five blocks to the edge of a catholic convent. The guys must have thought I would just run back to the school. I was looking for a box or anything to cover up with when a white van pulled up out of nowhere.

After a quick explanation of what was happening two somewhat inebriated local guys offered to give me a ride. They thought I was getting mugged or worse because a good deal of red paint had been added to the peanut butter party. So, I climbed in the back and they quickly lost the underpowered Falcon. Stopping at a home a mile or so away, they returned with a white sheet they said I could keep. Then they dropped me beside the school and I happily but quickly walked into the school and showered. It did take several days to get all the turtle wax out of my hair.

The same night, a black student named Mike stepped off his bus from work and got peanut buttered plus white shoe polish. However, evolution had just about run its course for the peanut butter tradition. The next day the Dean of Men issued a notice that the peanut butter tradition was officially ended and anyone participating would be expelled.

Jan and I married the summer of my junior year and studying at home and off campus helped my grades improve. It also helped to add a pair of eyeglasses for a stigmatism that I had no idea I had. Suddenly, I could comprehend much better. Still, I needed nearly perfect grades my last semester to graduate. Somehow, with God's help, I did graduate but was immediately challenged by another predicament.

It was the height of the Vietnam War and I received a notice to report to the Oakland Induction Center for the Army. Was it possible I was getting drafted? Entering the center, I was amazed at the number of young men reporting. After a short period, a blaring speaker announced the purpose of the gathering. Then a uniformed official wanted anyone with a note from their doctor to raise their hand. About three fourths of those present raised their hand. The letters were collected and those presenting them were excused. Then everyone lined up and a doctor or his assistant went down the line. One person would be asked to cough and a stethoscope was placed on their chest. The only problem was that this happened so fast that the stethoscope was on the next person before the last person coughed. I thought this very strange. One of the young guys told another he had a whole in his mouth and asked if that should keep him out. The doctors had apparently missed this. I did pass the exam and was given the classification II A which just meant I was a student and available for the draft. What was God's will for Jan and I now?

At the same time, I received my acceptance to Golden Gate Conservative Baptist Seminary in Mill Valley, California. I had packed four and one-half years into a four-year college program at Simpson and so my only class available that spring at the seminary was choir. I did use the semester to find the library. My wife and I had started attending our denomination's church in Oakland and worked in the children's church but had to commute from Daly City near South San Francisco. So, we moved to Oakland and I went to work for the church as youth director and assistant pastor on what was supposed to be a two-year internship program. When I began seminary, my draft status was changed to IV D. Just meaning I was a ministerial student. My mother had told me once that since all three of her brothers served in the military, she did not feel I needed to serve.

Two of my uncles, Sam and James Sardam, were in the Construction Brigade, more commonly called the CBs, and helped build the airport on Guam. They had to put up the blade on the bulldozers and could hear enemy sniper's bullets ping off the blades. My other Uncle, Porter Day, served in the Air Force and he was trying to out run an enemy patrol, when his Jeep rolled, and his legs were burnt severely. He was rescued and spent nearly a year in a hospital getting skin grafts. He was my favorite uncle because I would ask him to, "throw me up to the ceiling uncle P.B." I could not really say P.D. because of a childhood lisp. Then he would grab me and throw me up in the air, even with his stiff neck.

As it turned out, I never was drafted although I was willing to serve if God so directed. Jan was especially relieved because just prior to working for the church she had become pregnant. Although her previous job's insurance plan would pay for the birth, something (the Holy Spirit) told me we should have a thousand dollars saved just in case. As the time drew near for the baby to be born, he had not turned head down to be born naturally. The doctor quickly scheduled Jan for a caesarean birth. At the same time, the church and our families began praying and we prayed she would not need to have the operation. A couple nights later my wife went into labor and the doctor decided, because the baby was small, to have him be born backwards. All the nurses were called in to witness the unusual birth. To say I was scared would be an understatement, but I had some peace knowing a lot of people were praying. All we could do was pray and remember we were hardwired to the most powerful force in the universe.

Gowned up and observing the birth, my first thought was something went wrong as blood shot all over the wall. Soon, I learned this was to be expected. Then the doctor pushed the tiny feet up and gently twisted them out. It seemed like a long time as they cleaned out his mouth and then I heard his first cry. I could breathe again and so could the doctor and nurses.

Since it was not a caesarian birth and categorized a major operation, the insurance company would not pay the bill. We were more than happy to pay the thousand dollars that we had saved with no idea why we would need it. But we knew God was fully aware, and we both felt He would not leave us hanging. Our power source, and yes, I am talking about Jesus, had the perfect solution to our need. We just needed to stay close, remain faithful, and watch what only he could do.

Christopher David was born on Saint Patrick's Day and true to his name has been "Christ's bearer" ever since. He has been a mentor to hundreds of young people where he teaches literature at Klahowya High School in Silverdale, Washington. Recently, with the help of his New Life church, he and his wife, Rhonda, began a feast and forum time for his community in Seabeck, WA. They eat together, and then Chris gives a short message. After this, they discuss what he spoke about.

This may be closer to what would happen in the early church than what happens in many churches today. I will relate God working a miracle in his young life later.

Back to the the Pacific Northwest!

V.

Back to the Pacific Northwest

The church in Oakland had decided to offer the internship to more students and make it one year. At the same time we felt God calling us back to our roots in the Pacific Northwest. So, packing our meager belongings in a U-Haul truck, we headed north with my wife's sister and my brother-in-law driving our car behind us. The terrible economy had caused a huge gasoline shortage, and inflation was rampant. Sometimes, when we stopped for fuel, there was none. So, we had to hunt for an open station that had fuel, often waiting in a long line, hoping they would not run out. Somehow, we made it to Seattle but faced another big problem.

We stayed with Jan's parents to save money, but there were no jobs to be had. In fact, someone had placed a sign headed south on I-5 that said, "Will the last person leaving Seattle please turn out the lights." Funny? I suppose, but scary to a young family with three mouths to feed. With no open church jobs and not much in other marketable experience, I found looking for work exhausting and somewhat depressing. It was time to ask the Lord to guide us and it was not time for a pity party.

At last, a break came. My older brother had recently started a CPA firm and invited me to learn accounting from the ground up. Fortunately debits and credits came natural for me and I had taken bookkeeping in high school. Still, I felt inadequate compared to other accountants and took night school courses at a nearby community college to catch up.

VI.

Helping in a Rural Church

A college friend invited us to help in an American Sunday School Union Church that was in a rural community, called Selleck, just east of Tacoma WA. These churches, often too small to hire full-time pastors or staff, when added together, form one of the largest church organizations in all of America. This organization is now known as InFaith and was called the American Missionary Fellowship when I was ordained by them in 1975. We would drive about thirty miles with our family and hold Sunday School classes followed by a church service.

One woman had been praying over fifteen years for her husband to turn his life around. He was a tough, lumber truck driver, and was drinking himself into an early grave. Late one night he drove off the Kent-Kangley Road and right into a large tree. His legs were both broken and pinned under his car seat. He was bleeding, unconscious, and would have surely died if not for God's grace.

Down the same dark road came an aid car out on a different run. Barking dogs got an attendant's attention. They pulled over, found Don's vehicle, got him out, stabilized him on the way to the hospital. As a result, he turned his life over to Jesus. You might say he got his terribly short circuited life turned around and became hardwired to the person of Jesus Christ. He gave up drinking and began attending church with his wife and family. This type of experience caused me to realize that God never gets tired of our continual prayers for loved ones.

God had not turned a deaf ear to his wife's faithful prayers. Later, my wife and I would need this type of faith to endure the challenges ahead.

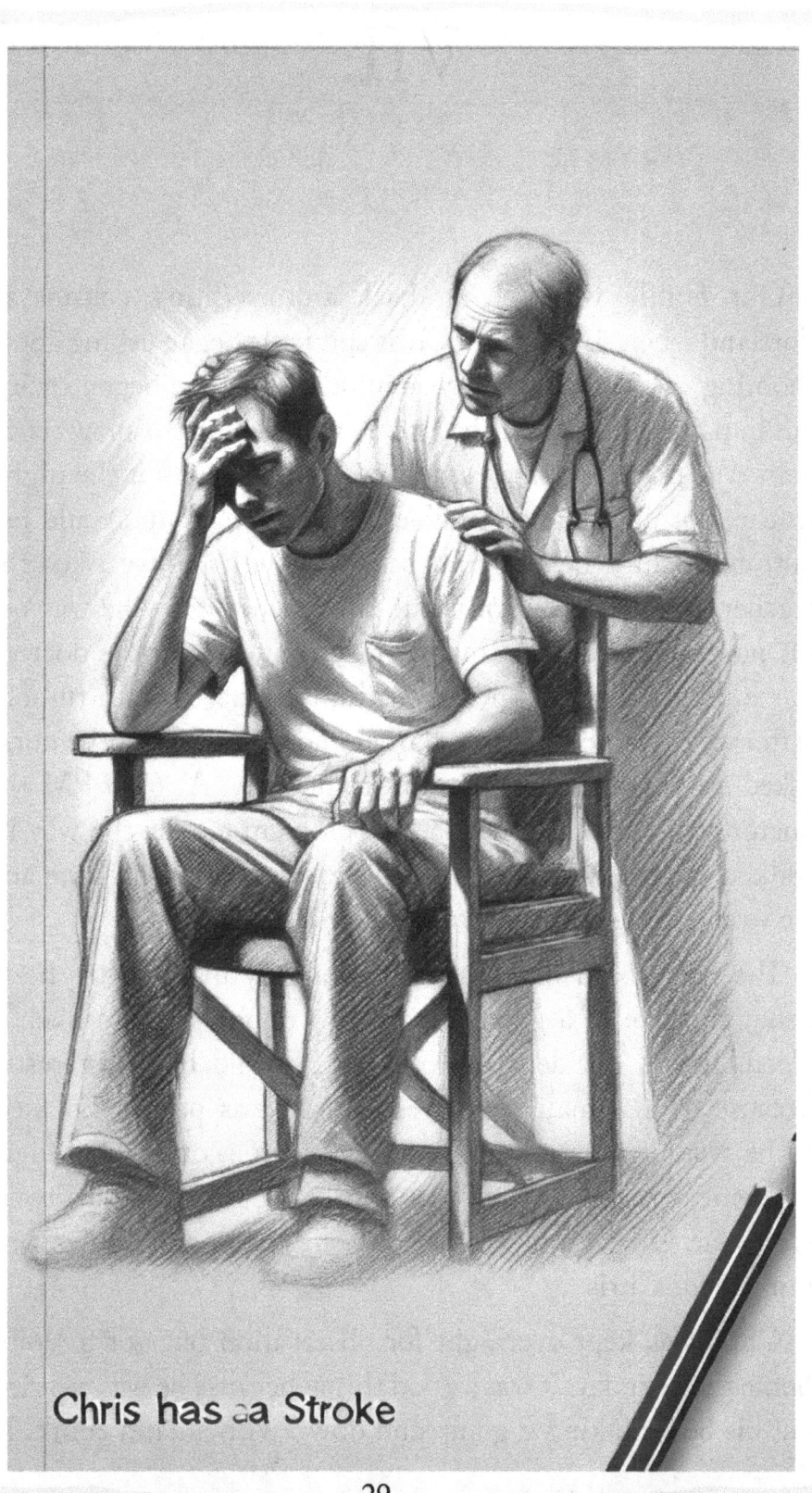

Chris has a Stroke

VII.

Chris Has a Stroke

Our family was driving back from visiting cousins in Portland when six-year-old Chris suddenly began asking about shooting stars. Problem: It was midday. Then he began crying out in pain with a headache. It was not like him to show much pain. We made it home, and quieted him down for the night. In the morning, he had trouble tying his shoes and could not button his shirt. He did go to school though and we asked the teacher to keep an eye on him. The teacher knew he was not his normal self and we finally made contact with the doctor's nurse. She said, "I suppose you think he has a brain tumor." After we explained his grandfather had died of ALS, the nurse asked for the doctor to see him right away. At 6:00 PM the doctor could tell he had a serious problem just by the way he walked. The UW had just added their first scan machine and we would know more after the Cat Scan.

The scan confirmed that he had a grey mass on his brain about the size of a golf ball. Not a tumor but more likely a bleed. It was decided that operating would be a last resort because of his small blood vessels. He was put on Dilantin so he would not stroke again. At the time, only about eight pediatric strokes occurred in the entire Pacific Northwest each year. Once again, we were on our knees, and asking for a miracle for Chris.

Chris was kept overnight for observation but got to come home the next day. It was a good thing, because he was wearing out his bed, making it go up and down with a hand crank. In three weeks, another scan confirmed his mass was the size of a pea. His doctor switched him off Dilantin, and put him on aspirin that he took for about one year. Our prayers had been answered again. Chris's personality quieted down greatly, and for several years he still had markings behind his ear where he could have been operated on, but God had different plans for him. Since he was otherwise healthy, he got to go home, and we really praised the Lord.

VIII.

Mount St. Helens

There is a Light Up Above

After becoming Director of a non-profit that gave ex-prisoners a second chance, I was asked to visit the State Penitentiary at Walla Walla and speak to a sociology class. Most of these prisoners had a GTD (Good time release date) within the next year and were anxious to hear anything that might help them adjust on the outside. The trip was set for mid-May of 1980 and we decided that this would be a great time to kill several birds with one stone. So, we combined the Friday trip to Walla Walla with a visit to my sister and other friends in Spokane. Jan and I and our three kids piled in the car and headed east. Not wanting to leave my family in the waiting room at the prison, I had them picnic in the city park while I spoke. All went well, and I encouraged about twenty prisoners that had families to find more than minimum-wage jobs when they returned home. I did so, because with another person back at home, they usually lost benefits yet had less money for the family to get by on. It was hard enough to find a job on the outside, but with the stigma of being a felon, it made it twice as hard.

After I picked up the family at the city park, we headed up through the state's three D's; Dayton, Dixie, and Dusty and eventually arrived at my wife's uncle's place near Colfax. Glen, many called him "whiskers," was a real-life cowboy and lived in a trailer home on his boss's ranch. It was a great visit because we did not get to see him or his two boys very often.

Then, it was on to Spokane to visit my sister and family and other friends.

After staying with my sister, we visited friends on Summit Boulevard overlooking the Spokane river. Then we noticed something strange. It looked as if a fastmoving storm was approaching from the southwest. We turned on a radio and learned that Mount St. Helens had exploded. The whole top of the mountain had been blown up into the sky and the debris was drifting east. Ash was falling as close as Wilbur, WA on the North interstate Highway. I had scheduled a board meeting and needed to get back to Seattle. Not realizing the magnitude of this event, we piled the family into the car, said some quick goodbyes, and thought we could surely outrun the storm.

Was I ever wrong! Soon trucks doing 80 and 90 miles per hour were trying to outrun the storm and blowing ash all over us. Jan was crying, "Turn around!" and the kids were echoing the same. Then I made an even worse mistake and hit the wash windshield button. The ash caked on the windshield, so I had to stop and scrape some off to see. Yielding to the screams inside the car, I did turn around, as the sun was setting on all four sides of us. I was able to follow a guardrail as my whole family prayed as we had never before. It was now pitch dark at 2:30 in the afternoon. And as ash fell like light snowfall, without divine help, my little family was about to perish.

We were traveling on a slight up-grade and then I saw something up ahead. We probably were doing only 5 or 10 mph, when a red light suddenly came into view through the falling ash. It was the only taillight on the back of a large truck and I was never so happy to be stuck behind a big truck in my life. We happily followed it and the guardrail all the way to the Maple Street bridge. On the bridge, the lamp posts gave us a little light, as we headed north, and were able to pass the truck. No sooner had we passed it than we almost hit a trailer with no lights and realized it was carrying a golf cart. After all, who needed taillights in the middle of a bright Sunday afternoon?

Our hosts were never so happy to see their idiot friends. We stayed with them for several days, as all the roads in and out of Spokane had closed. Finally, as news broadcasters were recommending, we stuffed an old t-shirt in our car's airduct to protect the engine from the ash as we traveled home the North highway. Once we reached the Columbia River, only a small trace of ash remained along the road.

My Mother journalized a lot of her prayers for her children. Later I read her prayer for our family when she knew the mountain had blown. She had written, "Lord Jesus, protect Dave and the family with a light from above and give them the time they can return home." Again, Jesus had heard all our prayers and intervened on our behalf.

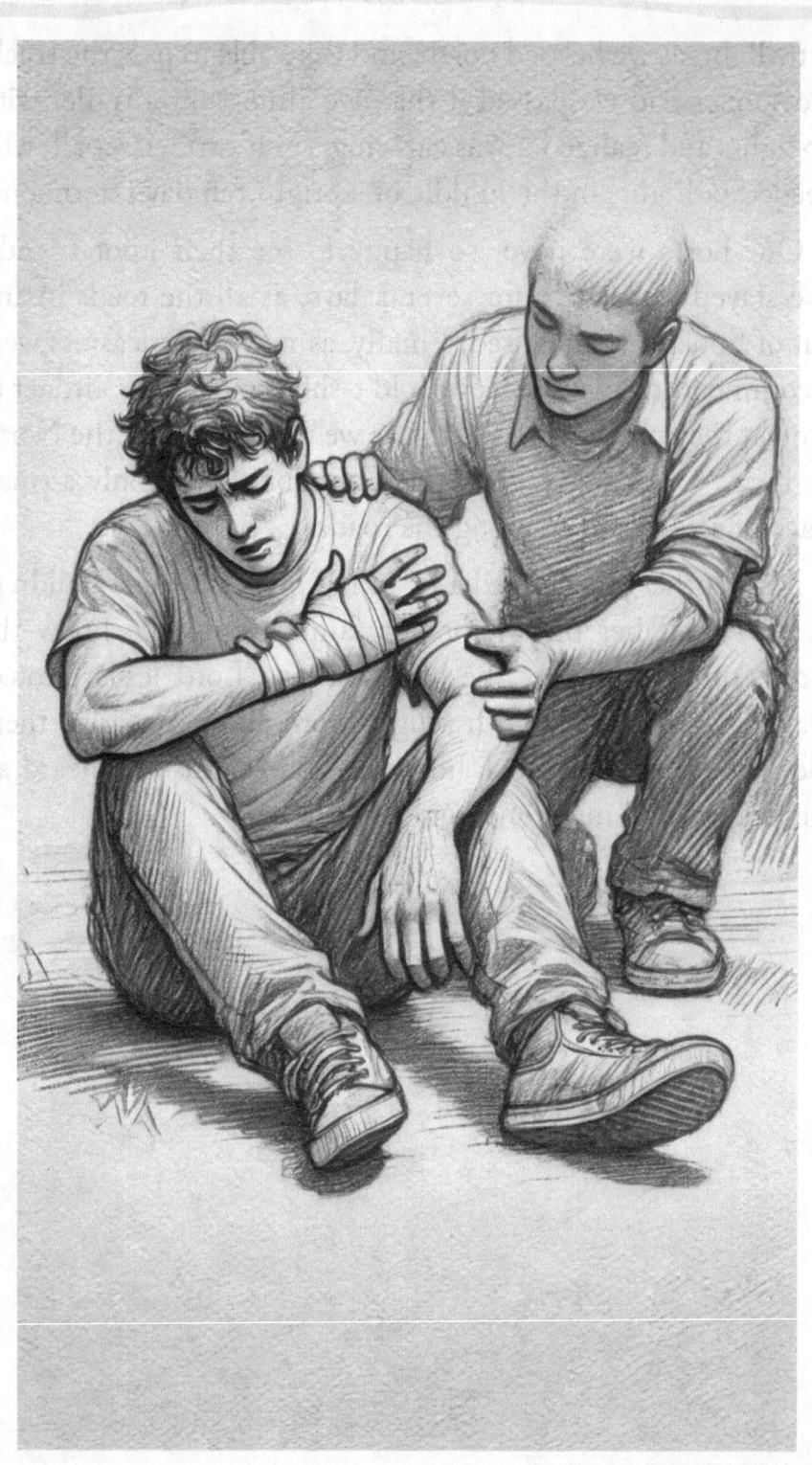

IX.

Shane Breaks a Wrist

In the Spring many young boy's hearts turn to off season football. This was the case with my youngest son, Shane William, who I often fondly refer to as Shanie Boy. As he was about to score a touchdown, he was tackled. He slammed his right arm into the ground to break his fall, and injured his lower arm near his wrist. It happened on a Sunday afternoon and I was home alone when I got the call. Jan was managing a stationary store, at the time, in downtown Seattle.

While driving to a hospital that turned out to be closed, I asked a rather dumb question, "How much does it hurt?" Shane's grimaced reply was, "Pretty bad." Soon, at Riverton Hospital Emergency, we were told he would need manipulative surgery. The procedure went as planned, and he was soon getting his friends' autographs on his cast.

There was a slight problem: Neither Jan nor I had a job that provided a family medical plan. Jan was very depressed, I was perplexed, and we both were poor as church mice. We had not forgotten how to pray, though. People began to give and the church's benevolent fund suddenly had enough to pay the entire bill. Jan's depression turned to tearful joy and thanks. I was no longer perplexed and we both realized how truly blessed and rich we were in Jesus.

X.
Cars for Missionaries Project

Soon after when I was helping our Church's District Men's Committee provide and maintain vehicles for furloughing missionaries, Shane and I teamed up to get a disabled vehicle back home. A missionary had broken down near Federal Way and we needed to get it back to West Seattle. The car was not running, so we would either have to have it towed or work out another solution. Thank goodness Shane was available, but I am not sure he had his drivers license just yet. Soon we were on our way to Federal Way and found the car. Shane climbed in and I pulled up the sedan and began pushing him home. We reached Des Moines after a few miles, and all was well. Then we spotted a police car and I motioned Shane to pull over into a donut shop. I must admit it was ironic, with all the jokes about police officers and donuts. We took a break, had a few donuts, and proceeded to make our way with a series of left and rights until we were home. This was just one of the many times we relied on our Lord for special assistance. Keeping hardwired into Jesus was becoming a family routine.

Not long after this the boys and I were traveling down what we called Boeing hill, in another vehicle, when all the brakes failed. I sensed that even the emergency brake was not going to stop us at the bottom. At the bottom was a narrow lane to avoid cars that were stopped, but I needed to jump the curb and cross over the side walk. Our guardian angels must have been working overtime, because we survived. All we heard was the blare of horns as we cut the corner and kept going. We did get the brakes repaired, but this vehicle had another problem. The alternator was not charging the battery. We decided to charge it with a trickle charger over night until we could afford the expensive alternator. We repeated this each night for well over two months, until one night the charger was stolen. Although we were not living in the remote Congo, one might get the impression that we were. We bought another trickle charger until we could get the alternator later. Through all this our faith in the Lord kept us going.

Another vehicle that we were getting back in shape was a two-toned Oldsmobile that the kids called "the gangster car." It had a broken engine mount and I was not sure what type of tool could help us get it repaired. It had to be a tool that could temporarily lift the engine so that the new mount could be slid in place. Now somewhere in my garage was about an eight-foot-long conduit bender. This turned out to be just the tool to leverage the engine long enough to do the replacement. The lesson Shane and I learned in this case was that sometimes God gives us unusual tools to accomplish His purposes.

Helping missionaries with their need for cars was only a voluntary project and it was at this time that I worked for the post office. One Christmas time I was clerking at the front counter in a suburb just south of Seattle. The station manager was dressed as an elf and was helping customers get oriented as they entered the office. It was two years after 9/11 and everyone was still reeling from that sad ordeal. The station manager brought over an elderly woman and said, "Dave can you help this kind woman with a package that has no zip code?

Taking a quick look at the package, I immediately realized a problem. The package was addressed to the Department of Defense, The Pentagon, but in Washington, D.C. "Oh", I told her casually, "I think the pentagon is actually in Arlington." BAM, down came her fist on the counter. "This package has the whereabouts of Osama bin Ladin", she declared. At this all the clerks were backing away from the front counter and the supervisors were headed forward. The station manager said something like, "I am sure we can find that zip code for you." One of the supervisors got on the phone and then told me give her 20002. Okay, so I told her that zip. She raised her voice again and said, "That is the zip code for Washington, D.C. and not Arlington. What is going on?" It took some time before she would relinquish her package to the station manager dressed like an elf, but she finally was satisfied and left.

Soon the head clerk returned from lunch and I told him about the excitement. "Oh," he laughed and said, "that was old Mrs. J. She lost her marbles some time ago". He continued, " I just take her news clippings about Bin Laden and give them back to her the next day. Last week she said he was in Italy."

It was somewhat of a relief when this temporary job ended. No other job I know of has your customers stand in a long line where they can observe everything you do and gang up to criticize your every move. My one takeaway: To error is very human and forgive divine. If nothing else, God was teaching me patience. I would need patience to deal with my wife's recurring tumor and a new problem that my daughter was about to confront.

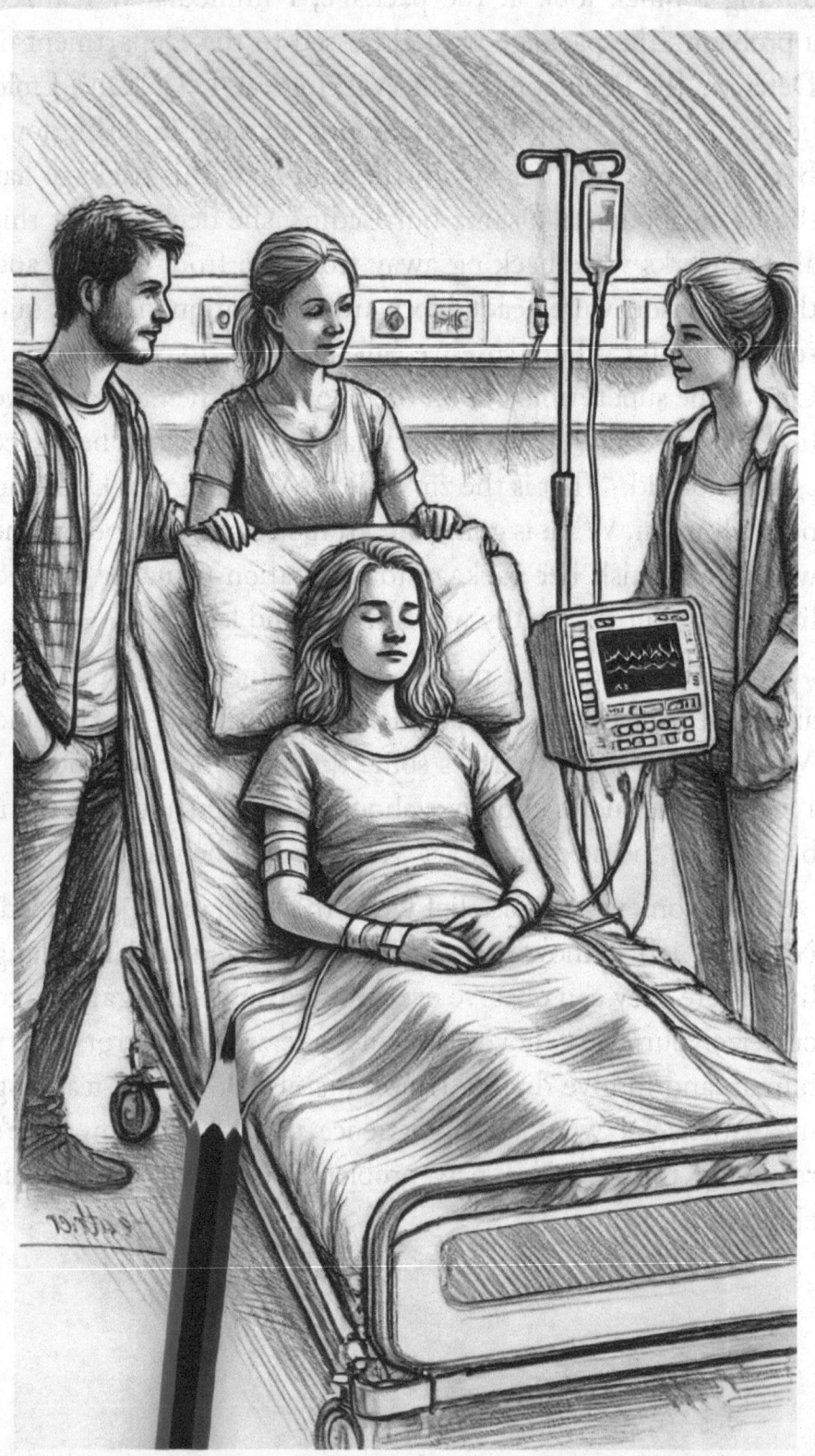

XI.

Heather's Miraculous Recovery From SCAD

My daughter, Heather Dawn, and her family were living at Lake Tapps, just a little Northeast of Tacoma, Washington. She was in a phone conversation with her close friend, Mary, when suddenly, she felt weird. Her heart began beating rapidly. She had not ever felt this way before. Mary remained on the phone long enough to get Heather's husband's work number and called her right back. They prayed together while he made the trip home from work. The consulting nurse said this sounded like something mechanical and they should go right to the emergency in Tacoma and get checked out. She felt a little better at the hospital but would stay overnight for observation.

This presented another problem. The baby, Jack Martin, was only a few weeks old and was hungry. Heather could not nurse him so Heather's husband went for formula. Heather asked for a bible and prayed during the night. In the morning her enzymes looked very unnormal. A heart catheter test would show any heart problems. Yes, there was a major problem. Heather had experienced a heart attack and now had something called SCAD. The emergency doctor on call happened to be one of the best heart surgeons in the area. He had seen this ten years earlier. A young woman had bled out before they could operate. They needed to get Heather into the OR right away because her heart arteries were erupting. Fortunately, the proper OR was available and the operation could start immediately.

At the time, I was working at a big hardware box store in Kent, WA that will remain nameless. After the call came, I left immediately for the hospital. It seemed like never in my life had I driven faster and prayed harder. When I arrived, Jan and I encountered Heather on the way to the operating room. She was crying and said she was scared. We were all scared and knew very little about SCAD (Spontaneous Coronary Artery Dissection). This was very serious and sometimes occurs after women give birth and their coronary artery linings separate. The TV actor, John Ritter, passed away from SCAD. Heather had six tears and had just had their fourth child, Jack Martin. We were all praying as we had at other times but with an intense sense of urgency.

Even though it was an emergency operation it would take three hours before we would hear any news. The surgeon finally emerged and said they had lost her heartbeat twice and had to restart it. She would be okay after recovering from the quadruple bi-pass surgery. With four children at home, we decided it might be best if she recovered at our house. Once again Jesus had answered our prayers and Heather quickly recovered.

A year later Heather ran a 10K at Point Defiance Park in Tacoma. I did an oil painting from a photo of her crossing the finish line with her arms raised in celebration. Praise God for her recovery and that we had hardwired Jesus into our lives, and even in a seemingly hopeless situation, he was working for our benefit. Today she is teaching kindergarteners at Bonney Lake, not all that far from Lake Tapps, and does not shy away from sharing her experience and faith.

XII.

Jan's Twenty-seven Year Ordeal

It was Labor Day weekend of 1997. This was the weekend that Princess Di was in a terrible crash in France that claimed her life. The headlines tended to obscure that Mother Teressa had also died over this weekend in India. My attention as well as our family and friends were focused on my wife who had begun having double vision. Tests revealed she had a brain tumor that was thought to be inoperable as it was too near her brainstem to operate safely. This tumor that grows out of the clivus (the bone the skull swivels on) was locally cancerous and does not normally spread to other organs. Once again, it was time to pray and realize Jan was hardwired to Jesus, the greatest physician in the universe. The one who specializes in everything.

Dr. Raisis not only administered the gamma surgery, but met with us after each MRI. At first there was a lot of observation and MRI's every six months. Jan's vision was getting worse and after two gamma knife surgeries (radiation) over the course of nine or ten years her right eye had moved completely toward her nose. The tumor had attacked her sixth nerve. Although one of the longest nerves in the head, and growing out of the pons just below the neck, it has a very singular function. It moves the eyes back and forth. It was Dr. Raisis that picked up a different problem. Jan had an aneurism near her carotid artery and would need to have a stint placed up through an artery as soon as could be arranged. Our previous pastor's wife had this done in Tacoma so we knew just who could do a good job.

Jan had the coiling procedure for this, and was recovering the next day at Tacoma General hospital. My daughter and her daughter, Molli, were visiting. Molli suddenly fainted, and hit the floor. All the nurses came running and Jan's surgeon soon followed. He was extremely happy to find out it was not because of Jan that they were headed to her room. Molli was treated in emergency and released in a couple hours. Doctor K. did a great job and once again we praised the Lord.

Despite all the previous times Jesus had come to our rescue, I could not help wondering what God had in store for us next. Yes, I knew everyone at church and in our family were praying for Jan, but just how many times would, or could He come through. We were about to find out just how great a God we serve.

Jan had learned to close her right eye when she turned her head so she would not see double. She had to do this for about two years. She saw an eye surgeon and it was confirmed the sixth nerve was not going to get any better. It was time to stitch her muscle in her right eye, allowing her to turn her head to see to the right while her left eye turned to the left more normally. Dr. M was exceedingly pleased with the outcome. Again, we praised the Lord. By this time, though, I was pretty used to thinking what next. Sure enough, within two years another challenge surfaced.

We were in Salt Lake City on a vacation trip to the national parks in Utah, when Jan complained that she was having angina and wanted me to pound on her back. Most families would think this to be an unusual request but this was the Seidel family after all. After stopping to rest a bit she felt better. Upon returning to Seattle, we had her checked out and she indeed had a severe hiatal hernia and most of her stomach had somehow been pulled up through her diaphragm. She would need surgery to pull her stomach back down. Once again, we prayed for Jan's recovery and my back after sleeping on a hospital couch overnight.

Since I had attended Seattle University for my Masters Degree in Public Administration, and it was right across the street from Swedish Hospital, I knew where all the good coffee shops were. God's mercies are new every morning, but God was not through working out his will for Jan. This procedure was only a bump in the road for Jan.

It had now been about seventeen years since Jan's first tumor diagnosis. Jan was beginning to get tired of the constant six-month MRIs to check on the tumor's growth and wished it could just be removed. Then one day Dr. Raisis called to say that there was a new skull base surgeon at Harborview hospital who could do a craniotomy operation and we should meet with him to see if Jan was a candidate. Any more radiation was ruled just too risky. After meeting with this neurosurgeon, he felt her tumor was not a meningioma but a rare chordoma and if he did not operate it would take her life. We again began praying as we had many times before. Not our will for Jan but your will Jesus our Lord and healer.

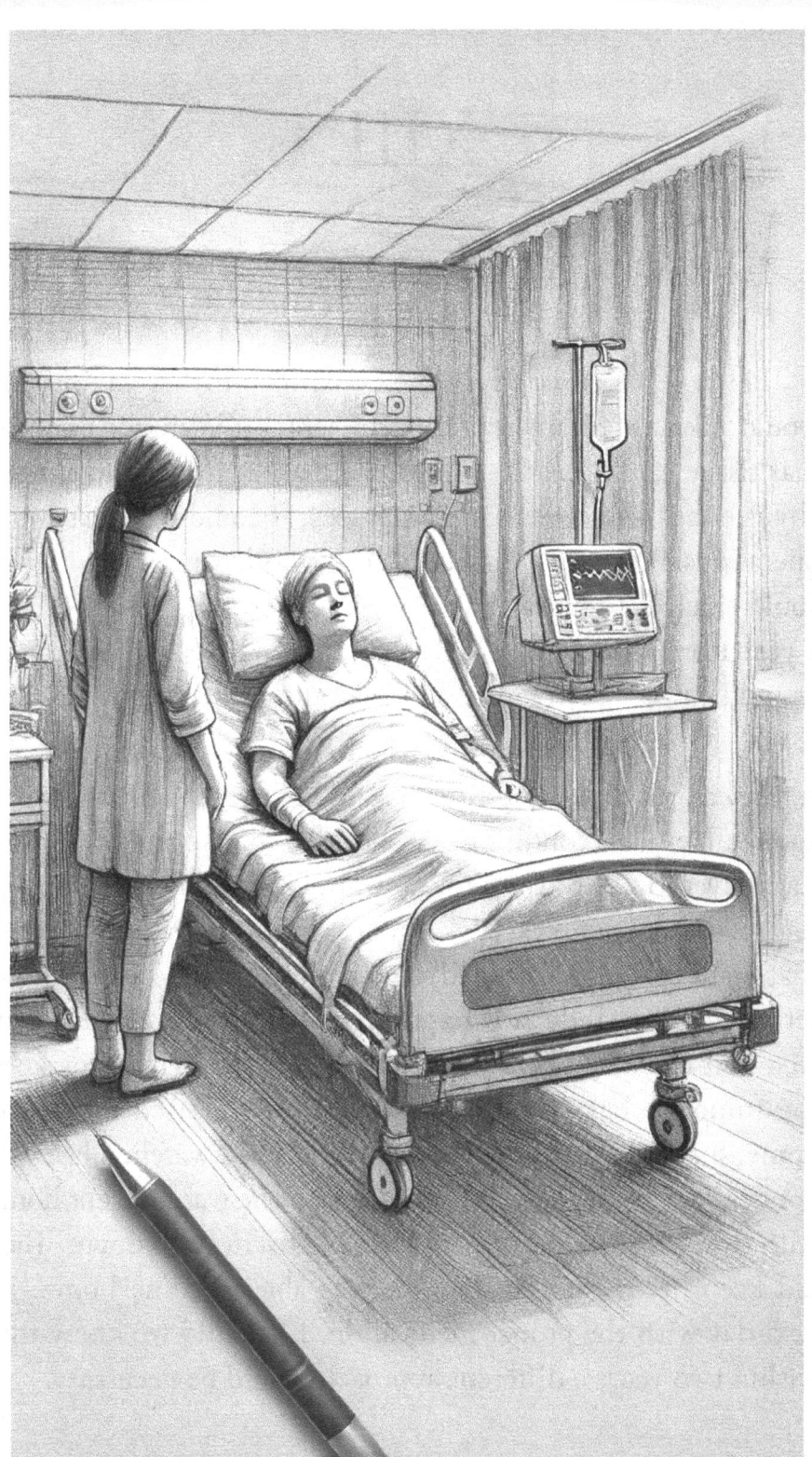

XIII.

The Surgeries

This type of tumor and the proximity to her brain stem would take a delicate operation to scrape the tumor and any scar tissue caused by the previous radiation treatments off the clivus bone. There were no guarantees. It could require several operations. We were thrilled that a good part of the tumor could safely be removed along with much scar tissue. About a year later, the routine MRI proved that a second operation would be necessary. Time to pray as always before.

We had been planning a trip to the East Coast, but air travel was out of the question, because of how the high altitude could affect Jan's condition. We decided to take the train from Vancouver B.C. to Toronto, and Dr. S. gave us the name of several other skull-based surgeons in Toronto and Boston that could help us if needed. The trip was wonderful, and we returned rested and ready to proceed. The second surgery went well and we once again praised the Lord for helping us keep the tumor at bay. The same day Jan was released and came home, she had a seizure. Chris called 911 as I watched Jan. We got her back to the hospital, and learned she was not sent home with the proper medication to keep her brain swell down. They did keep her overnight, but she was able to come home the next day with the proper medication. Little did we know that within two years a different approach would be necessary.

Some might think that once a tumor is removed it could not recur, but not so with this type of chordoma. It was locally cancerous and aggressive. The only good thing was that it did not tend to metastasize to other parts of the body. The tumor showed some growth in a slightly different direction and it was decided to have Jan's upper palate lowered and Dr. S. would go down through this space, just below the nose, and scrape the other side of the clivus bone. This was the most delicate of the three operations. It required two different types of surgeons working as a team. We all prayed as we had before but like never before. All went well. This longer operation took more time for recovery. God was again very good to us. Once more, the tumor had been held at bay, but should it return later, no more surgeries were advisable.

XIV.

Jan's Seizure and Broken Clavicle

After Jan's third surgery, we had been home about a week when I heard a strange gurgling noise coming from our back bathroom. There were some common "Jan noises" that I had grown accustomed to, but this sound was unique. I ran, only to find Jan hanging on the bathroom door handle. Before I could get to her, she had crashed like a tall tree, "boom," right outside the bathroom.

By now I had learned all the signs of a seizure, and this was certainly one of them. A few weeks earlier, I had taken a CPR class offered at Arbor Heights Community church. My CPR training went into full application. I got 911 on the phone immediately. They told me to hold the phone to her mouth and to begin chest compressions right away. I did so and began the "1-2-3-4 staying alive, staying alive" compression routine. Within minutes, the fire department was at the door. They went into full action with just the minimum questions. The fireman said fortunately the traveling hospital was in the area. It arrived in just ten minutes. They set up shop in our kitchen, and said I had done all the right things for Jan and she was stabilizing. She did not hit her head but had broken her right clavicle. An ambulance took her to the ER at Harborview Hospital, and I followed at a much-slower speed.

A good number of people in the ER were being treated for COVID-related illnesses. One man had had a broken beer bottle shoved in his ear by a distraught woman friend on First Avenue. Because the medical team could not find the source of the bleeding, they called in more and more help. After about three hours, a doctor finally saw Jan and told us they were full up for the night. So, he arranged for Jan to be transferred to the University of Washington Hospital. We were happy to get back home the next day and praised the Lord again for watching out for Jan.

They put Jan on an anti-seizure steroid called Keppra. The full significance of her not being able to endure any more surgery did not really sink in for us until we were told that the tumor was growing again. The oncologist suggested we try chemotherapy, and Jan began taking a drug that ultimately proved not to help. Another drug called Stutent had proved to be effective for pancreatic cancers and worked to stimulate the immune system into action. The side effects gave her blisters on the soles of her feet and some in her mouth. With no noticeable improvement after six months, we discontinued Stutent for the summer.

About this time Jan lost the use of one of her vocal cords. Her ear, nose, and throat specialist did not know if her growing tumor or an earlier small stroke had been the cause. He performed two procedures that helped considerably, and at the same time she began speech therapy. The exercises strengthened her diaphragm, and she learned new ways to swallow. Through all this we continued to consult the Lord for strength and guidance. The main concern was that food could get ingested into her lungs and then pneumonia could develop.

A follow-up scan showed she was able to avoid this. Again, we praised the Lord for answering our prayers.

A friend had suggested taking papaya juice, but we had been to four stores and none of them had the juice. Something told me to try one more store. In the back of a Safeway store, we seldom go to, we found our friend, Peli, and he said, "just buy the Papaya, add a little lemon juice, and make your own." We did and it has made a real difference in Jan's voice and swallowing. When you are hardwired to Jesus, the Holy Spirit will direct you to resources you may find surprising.

XV.

Goodbye Equinox and Hello Prius

Not long after this we had just finished a bible study at our friends' house when a close call nearly put me in the hospital or worse. After the meeting, a group member with disabilities needed a ride. Standing on the street side of our Equinox, I was leaning across the back seat to help her buckle in. Suddenly, I heard a horn and crashing. A car had careened around the corner and caught the edge of my open door behind me, and crushed it into the center pillar. It happened so fast, I had no time to think about what had just happened. Just a couple inches closer and I could have lost my legs or worse. Once again, we felt relief that no one was injured, and that being hardwired into Jesus meant He could protect us from a near catastrophe we could not see coming. A few days later our Equinox was totaled by the insurance company. I was not too disappointed by this because it was using about a gallon of coolant every few days. Shortly before this happened, I had prayed that the Lord would direct us as to what to do with the car. Now it was gone and we were eager to find out what the Lord had in store for us.

We needed a vehicle that would accommodate two ladies we often took to church-- one from Puerto Rico and one from Mexico. After a few days searching the internet, two vehicles appealed to us. Both dealers (in Bellevue and Auburn) were a good distance from our home in West Seattle. We looked at a nice Nisan SUV in Bellevue but wanted also to look at the

Prius wagon in Auburn. As we were driving to Auburn my wife got a call from her nephew, Duffy. Now Duffy does not call very often and lives with his family on the other side of the state. We were traveling to Duffy's Auto Brokerage which had no family affiliation. Wow, what were the chances? The salesman we met there was originally from Puerto Rico and had been a jockey at one time when the track was in Renton. One day the horse he was riding broke both front legs, and he was severely injured and in a comma. His parents were in Puerto Rico and could not be reached. The hospital needed permission to operate but if they could not get permission, they would operate anyway the next morning to drain blood from his head. During the night blood drained from his ear and he came out of the comma. He needed multiple operations, but he survived. It was not as if God had spared his life to sell us a vehicle that would help transport another Puerto Rican to church and bible study. Nevertheless, that is what happened. We did not need any other stars to align so we bought the Prius wagon.

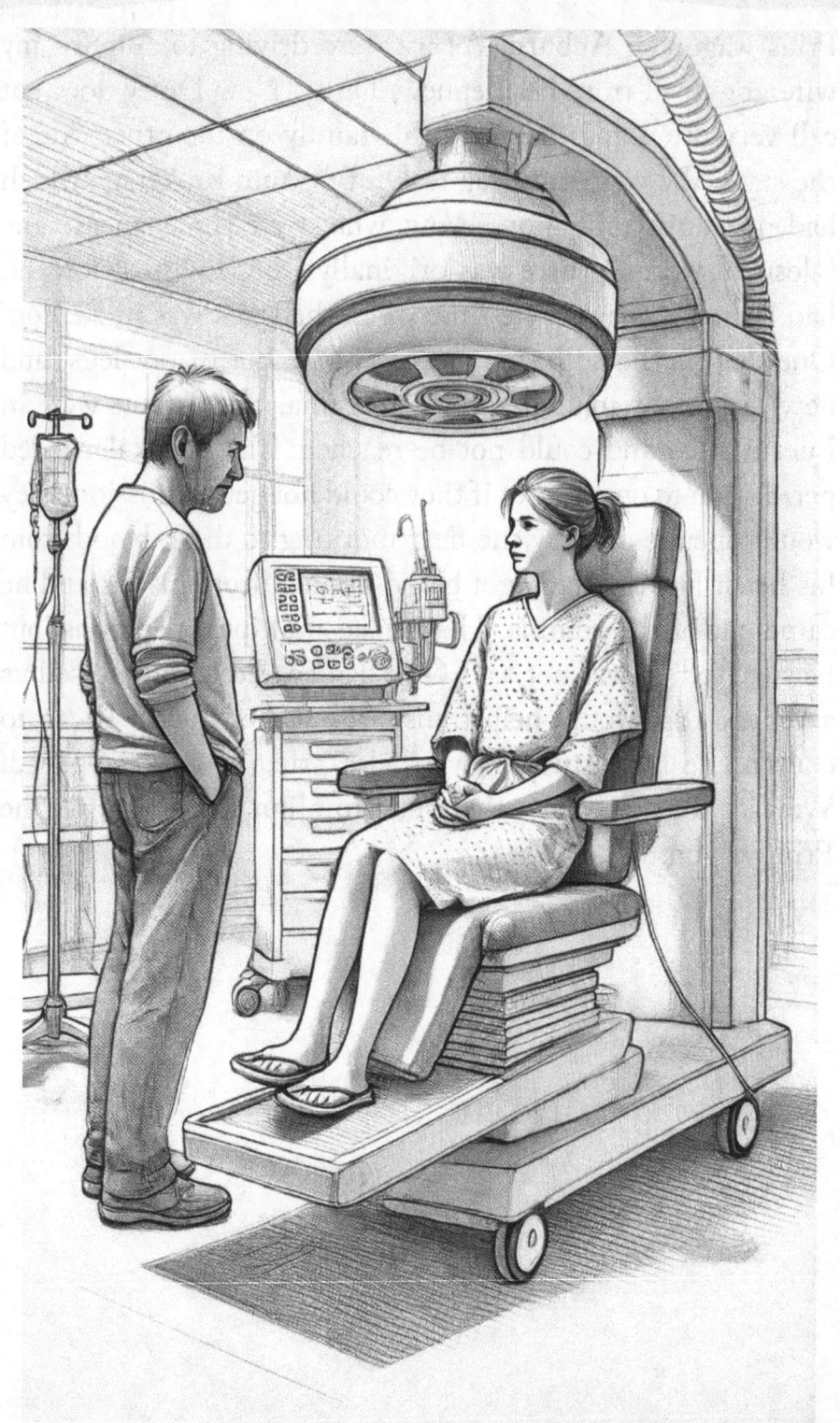

XVI.

Proton Therapy for Jan and Dave's Need for Surgery

In the fall, Jan was referred by Fred Hutch Cancer Center to Northwest Hospital for proton therapy. Fred Hutch and UW hospital had together funded a $150-million facility at Northwest hospital just to treat cancer patients with the proton beam. Because it had been about nine years since Jan's previous gamma knife procedures, she was a candidate for this more directed type of radiation. It would take 39 treatments, Monday through Friday, for six weeks. Again, we prayed and sought the Lord's will. Our church family volunteered to help drive, because I found out in mid-November, I had my own medical problem to overcome.

Jan and I enjoyed walking several times a week through Lincoln Park in West Seattle. But I needed to stop and catch my breath what seemed way too often. One night, finding myself short of breath, I went to the ER for a checkup. They ran an EKG test that I passed but they suggested I see a cardiologist to be sure. After failing the treadmill test, and having a heart scan, I was scheduled for a cardiac catheterization. It revealed 80+ percent blockages in the arteries in my heart. We prayed, and I felt like what the Israelites of the Old Testament must have felt. We seemed hemmed up against the Red Sea with pursuing chariots right on our heels. It was not an emergency like my daughter Heather had had, but it would be if not attended to soon. When I checked the on line MyChart system it told me I had an enlarged left ventricle and severe blockage.

We conferred with Dr. L. who was the same surgeon that operated on Heather 16 years earlier. He said I would need a quadruple bypass surgery. It was scheduled for November 14. We made plans. Our younger son, Shane, would come from California for the operation, and we would celebrate Thanksgiving as a family a week early. I might even be home for actual Thanksgiving Day.

A few days before we were planning to go in for the surgery, my appointment was taken by someone who needed an emergency heart valve replacement. The hospital rescheduled my operation for the following Tuesday—during Thanksgiving week. They say, "Life is what happens when we have made other plans." When we walked into Heather's house for our early celebration, Shane was there and surprised us. It was a wonderful surprise but the operation was a week away. We all had to make some adjustments and reschedule things.

We had made it through the "Red Sea" of our problems, but I was still very apprehensive about undergoing a surgery that would leave me needing physical therapy well into the new year. Jan's proton treatments would begin the second day of January, and I would not be able to drive her until the middle of February. This is when our church family went into action.

Nine drivers volunteered to help Jan get to the Northwest Hospital for her one-hour proton treatments. Sometimes this had to be done during the worst of commuter times and we will always be grateful to those who gave of their time and resources to help us.

It has now been about seven months since her last treatment in early March, 2024, and the side effects have only been minimal. Her problem of swallowing and lack of appetite has led to a big weight loss but we would not recommend losing weight this way. Her follow up showed that the center of the tumor was completely black (a good sign) with the outer part only a narrow white line of some swelling (another OK sign). Jan has again signed up for bible study fellowship this fall and we are both studying the book of revelation. Besides being "hardwired" to Jesus, we want to better understand why we are "ready to go".

PART TWO

XVII.

Dave's "Tunnel Vision"

My experience in the hospital recovering from heart surgery was not a return from death type one. After all I had just had a successful operation. It was, however, more vivid, and seemingly real than any dream I have ever had. The term "tunnel" is only used because most people can relate best to this terminology. With this understanding it is best to just launch into what I experienced.

It all began on Tuesday November 21, 2023 when I was admitted for necessary multi-bypass coronary surgery. Had the surgery taken place a week earlier, as originally planned, I would have been home for Thanksgiving. But a heart valve patient needed the appointed time and OR facility more than I did. As mentioned earlier, Jan's health issue made me very apprehensive. My actual operation went very well, and instead of four by-passes only three were necessary to eliminate the 80+ percent blockages.

When I awoke, it seemed as if I were in a very crowded room with a guard seated in front of me. Many people dressed in black were milling around. Hardly hospital garb, I thought. The guard told me they were fascists. For some reason, I felt I needed to get to the airport and told him so. I started to remove my IV's and catheter, he quickly stopped me, saying I could injure my bladder if I continued.

Hallucinations are common for those coming off anesthetics and other drugs post-op. The next morning my son reassured me that all the people at the hospital were there to help me. That gave me great comfort. Linet, an evening nurse, also gave me comforting advice. She said, "David, Jeremiah 29:11 (NIV) is yours. For I know the plans I have for you. Plans to prosper you and not to harm you, plans to give you hope and a future." Later I read vs.12 which really spoke to me. It says, "Then you will call on me and come and pray to me, and I will listen to you. You will find me when you seek me with all your heart."

The one big obstacle I faced was lack of sleep. The direct line in my throat was uncomfortable, caused when I tried to remove it while hallucinating. After two nights of little sleep, a night nurse noticed my discomfort and said he could now remove it and put two IVs on my wrist. I told him I would be very grateful and reward him with a cigar (Half jokingly). He said he preferred whiskey, and I said go for it (Not jokingly).

He told another younger nurse to get a surgery kit. She did so, and he instructed her how to cut the adhesives that held the direct line in my neck. She was scared, but he said she needed to learn this step. She was over the moon that it went so well. He then removed from my neck the long needle that resembled a narrow pea pod. He then put two others in the top of my wrist. Later, when I came back for a checkup, I kept my part of the bargain, and brought a bottle of Kentucky Bourbon, from Trader Joes's, for his off-duty use.

Thanksgiving turkey never tasted so good, even on Friday and even in the hospital. It was the first time in several days I ate the whole meal (except the cranberries). About this time, one of the nurses asked, if I was concerned about anything at home. I explained about Jan's tumor without taking her through the whole 26 years. I guess I sort of broke down, because who was going to take care of Jan if anything were to happen to me? She gave me some great counsel and said, "God never will give us more than we can handle." She also gave me a device that showed my heartrate when I pushed some buttons, and that night I slept soundly after checking my heartrate about ten times.

Each night, in cardio intensive care, a person sits with you in case you need special care. A student nurse named Valarie sat with me one night. As we talked she showed me a picture of her beautiful five children, including twin eleven-month-old boys. After several restless nights with that crooked toad-stabber (direct IV line) in my neck, it was good to drift off to sleep. It was in the middle of that night that I had an amazing vision.

PART THREE
THE TUNNEL VISION

XVIII.

Love Sent Me Back

The vision I saw was more like a tall yellowish closet than a typical round white tunnel reported by some. I do not remember stepping on stairs, but I saw some as I was going forward toward a large window. Through the window I could see a bright morning sky with brilliantly shining stars. It was the most beautiful sky I have ever seen. Out of a mist, I immediately saw my Lord Jesus. I reached for Him and merely said, "help me." Somehow, I knew that he understood my need.

He spoke strongly and firmly, "You have come far but I'm sending you back to help your wife." He placed his hand on my shoulder and turned me around. Then I was back in my room and he was no longer there. I felt a warm heat move through my chest and I knew I was going to be okay. The clock above my bed was illuminated by the TV on the opposite wall. It said 2:30AM and I asked Valarie if I could call the night nurse for a gas pill. For some reason I asked her if she had a church or temple. She said no but she was going to go to church now. Christine, the night nurse, was a real angel. She found me a gas pill and then said to go back to sleep. I could hardly wait till morning. Who would I tell first?

XIX.

Going Home

Before breakfast, eager to walk, I made about ten laps around the nurses' station with my new-found strength. After breakfast I did another seven laps, and the dayshift nurses coming on their shifts were quite impressed. They felt I would likely be discharged by afternoon.

After lunch, it was great to get my drainage tubes, electrodes, and IV out. After I "dropped my last potato" (cardio lingo for using the potty), vitals were taken, and it was time to dress, get my pharmacy order, and final instructions. Jan and granddaughter, Rachel, were there to pick me up.

During my first week home from the hospital, another granddaughter, Grace Elizabeth, came from Colorado and provided wonderful help. Gracie is a pharmacist, and I received excellent medical advice, and we also shared some great stories and humor. We even came up with a new game called mix Papa's "Bismark juice" (laxative). For those who are unfamiliar with the Bismark. It was the largest and fastest battleship the Germans had at the beginning of WWII. In the 1960's a young recording artist, Johnny Horton, had a hit record called "Sink the Bismark". Need I say more.

Gracie could only stay for about a week and had to return to her job in Denver. This is when Heather would come everytime I needed to refill my pill dispenser, and for the next six weeks helped me sort it all out. After sixteen years, she still recognized some of the same heart medications that she once took.

XX.

The Zoom Meeting
Grace Adult Class

Not long after I was home from the hospital, my brother-in-law, a writer and retired pastor, asked if I would relate my hospital "vision" experience to a national group interested in such encounters. He meets regularly with these eight or nine individuals from Lacey, WA to southern Florida.

Larry was kind enough to get the meeting all set up. I related exactly what I had experienced, which was much more real and vivid than any dream I had ever experienced before or since.

Should you wish to view this meeting it is on the internet site:

https://youtu.be/brYU-4sFmFI.

Larry has a sense of humor also, but not quite as extreme as my brother-in-law Ken. So, if you hear part of Handel's Messiah at the beginning you are on the right site.

AND MY ♥ WOULD BE OK.

HAD HEALED MY SPIRIT
I HAD A FEELING JESUS
MOVE THROUH MY CHEST
AND FELT A WARM HEAT
NO LONGER THERE. I AWOKE
ME AROUND. THEN HE WAS
SHOULDER AND TURNED
PLACED A HAND ON MY
HELP YOUR WIFE". HE
YOU'RE GOING BACK TO
"YOU HAVE COME FAR, BUT
WAS STRONG AND FIRM
MY LORD JESUS! HIS VOICE
I KNEW, AT ONCE, IT WAS
WITH BRIGHT SHINING STARS,
MORNING BLUE SKY,
OUT OF A BRILLIANT

XXI.

The Sketch and Painting

My youngest son has had a great deal of art education and training and he has won a good number of contests from high school to graduate school including the Hayward Prize. This even allowed him to study performance art in Austria. Before all this, and while he was still in high school, I was looking for my high-top sneakers to play basketball with the usual guys. I found they had been painted gold and placed on a five-gallon bucket. On top was a miniature resemblance of a Michael Jordan looking figure dunking a basketball, all made from coat hanger wire. I was able to play that local game with the gold shoes but they never became a rave.

For either a Father's Day or birthday, Shane had given me some art supplies. He knew that back in college and seminary I had taken an art class. So, I was able to sketch out my hospital "tunnel" vision. Since then, I have completed the oil painting of what I experienced. He also gave me the idea of telling what I experienced on the bottom of the canvas from the bottom up. If the picture of my painting is in this manuscript just remember that I am no Picasso.

XXII.

Aftermath

It has now been over seven months since Jan's last proton treatment, and her side effects have been minimal. Jan's ARNP has put her on an ice cream diet so she can gain weight. Some of her friends are envious. A few weeks after her last proton treatment, Jan had a cat scan of her throat to rule out a potential problem her proton doctor saw. MyChart results came back with a lump on her throat that was cancerous. At first, we were devastated. We mustered up courage to place Jan in God's perfect care again. We were to meet with her proton doctor the next day. When we walked in, we saw David, the Doctor's Assistant, who could not be happier. He said that MyChart was wrong and Jan only had swollen glands. Once again, we could not be more relieved. How could we have doubted our hardwired connection to Jesus. There was no disconnect. In October, 2024, Jan will have a follow up MRI and we are trusting the Lord for good results.

Meantime, my health has been steadily getting better and I have completed all the in-hospital cardio physical therapy. At my first cardiologist follow up I asked if my heart would reduce its size? He said that sometimes the MyChart system forecasts a wrong impression. MyChart was wrong and my left ventricle was not ever enlarged. I only had blockages. We both have joined a YMCA for additional physical workouts.

God certainly has been good to us and we both are fortunate to have great medical teams, great friends, and a loving creator.

As a reward for completing all her proton therapy, Jan and I attended a Lauren Daigle concert at the Washington State Fair. This was especially meaningful because during her 39 treatments she would listen to a Lauren Daigle CD. We were sitting high up in the arena listening to Lauren's opener, Blessing Gofor, as he ministered in music to a big crowd. It was a beautiful evening and I looked up and saw the Good Samaritan hospital on the Puyallup hillside. I thought to myself, "I should get ahold of my friends Bryan and Cheryl who live here in Puyallup." Bryan had wrestled with heart related health issues the past few years. My phone then buzzed and I had a text message.

It was Bryan's son, Kyle. He said that Bryan had passed away that morning. I was just stunned the whole concert, but by the end the Holy Spirit through Blessing, Lauren, and the tour staff had ministered to my soul in a wonderful way. Some other close friends informed us of the service for him and we attended three weeks later.

The testimonials for Bryan revealed someone who was definitely hardwired into his Lord and Savior. His earthly vocation was wood products salesman, but his heavenly calling was to talk to people. Frequently he would stop in at two or three Starbucks just to meet new people. Some of these had troubles. Bryan counselled and helped all kinds of people. He didn't shrink from being a loving husband and father of three great children and four grands. Yes--Bryan was "ready to go" and enjoy the joy of his master.

XXIII.

Conclusion

The Bible records what the Apostle Peter explained to a confused Jerusalem crowd when the Holy Spirit came at Pentecost (Acts 2:16 and 17). Those receiving the Holy Spirit were not drunk. Instead, explained Peter,

"No, this is what was spoken by the prophet Joel:

In the last days, God says, I will pour out my Spirit on all people. Your sons and daughters will prophesy. Your young men will see visions, your old men will dream dreams."

Pastor and author Mike Pickard in his devotional book, *Rediscover the Bible or Discover it for the First Time*, writes, "The Holy Spirit comes upon the disciples in dramatic fashion, giving them the ability to speak in the native languages of all the people that were present for the feast of Pentecost from all over the region."

God only knows when Jesus will return to take us to heaven, but we are closer every day. I only know that what I experienced was more real than any dream I have ever had before or since. I must admit, I had my doubts about "tunnel visions," but I will never doubt anyone's similar experience again.

Peter also quoted Israel's King David, vs. 25, when he said, "I saw the Lord always before me. Because he is at my right hand I will not be shaken." Peter's address must have been convincing because about 3000 people were added to the faith that day.

My witness is this. That late one night Jesus turned me around physically, spiritually, and emotionally and one day I fully expect to see him again. There is no better way to light up your life than to be hardwired into Jesus. When we seek him with all our heart, he will come to us. He is waiting to hear our cry or our whisper.

Sometimes I have been tempted to wish God would just completely heal Jan's tumor. After all, he certainly is capable and all powerful. Then I must remember what God's servant Job said, after his wife told him to curse God and die. "Am I to accept only the good from God and none of the trouble." (Job 2:9-11 NIV). Writing this and relating God's goodness to our family and many friends has caused me to realize, with the Holy Spirit's help, that is exactly what he has been doing the last 27 years. Granted he has used a good number of doctors and specialists to accomplish his purposes. In fact, I am told this chordoma probably has been with Jan from the time she was in her mother's womb. God certainly has had complete control over it and will continue to do so.

As Watchman Nee, the great Chinese Christian pastor, theologian, evangelist and martyr for his faith has stated, "Good is not always God's will, but God's will is always good." Watchman Nee firmly believed that God's Holy Spirit lived in his heart. He certainly got plugged in at an early age and then remained "hardwired" to Him the rest of his life. After twenty years behind bars in a communist labor camp in China he died and was rewarded with heaven.

It is both Jan and my prayer that, whatever your stage in life, that you will trust Jesus, if you have not already, and remain "hardwired" to Him. He has made all the difference in both our lives and is always waiting to hear from you. Someday, looking up into his big beautiful brown eyes, I want to hear from his strong and firm voice like Matthew 25:11 (NASB). "Well done good and faithful servant, enter the joy of your master."

Seven Take Aways

- If your father cusses you out, remember he is still your dad.
- (He may need a savior like everyone else).
- Never put your head near an open locker.
- Sometime you may need more than one spare tire.
- Keep the faith, but don't pretend to.
- It's okay to ask for help. SOS doesn't stand for Stuborn Or Stupid.
- Trust completely in Jesus, but not always, MyChart.
- If your wired into Jesus you will be ready to go.

The End

Works Cited

Michael Pickard, *Rediscover the Bible or Discover it for the First Time*, Poulsbo, Washington, Kitsap Publishing, 2017, p.582

Watchman Nee, Ni Tuosheng, en.wikipedia.org/wiki/Watchman_Nee

Works Cited

Michael Pollard. *Red Scarves in a Sea of Blue*, city of the First Zine Boutito, Washington, Kinsey Publishing, 2012.

Watchman Lee, Nii Tuochang, core.depository/wfs, Watchman Lee.